I0420795

BIPOLAR DISORDER

by
Penni Less

Copyright 2015 Denise Funaro
All Rights Reserved

ISBN 978-1517183806

Proceeds from the sale of this book will go to helping
fund mental health research.

Published by BeelinePublishing.com
Tequesta, FL

CONTENTS

DEDICATION

INTRODUCTION

THIS BOOK IS DEDICATED TO MY THREE WONDERFUL CHILDREN.

To my dear sweet daughter Toni who took her life two weeks before her 35th birthday. It will hopefully enlighten the need for understanding, caring and mostly erasing the stigma of mental illness.

To my darling daughter Dana who has lost her best friend and has been my strength, encouragement and hope through this terrible tragedy. For showing me what a wonderful, thoughtful adult she has become.

To my son Michael who lost his second mother and had his own issues. He dealt with his issues and has become an amazing, caring, supportive source in my life. Because of mental illness his whole college curriculum had to change, yet he persevered!

To my son and daughter in laws who have been so supportive and loving to me and my children.

To my grand-daughter whom I hope will learn how much her mother loves her and had no control of her illness.

To my son in law who has had a traumatic life altering event, as we all have, that will haunt him forever. I hope he will accept our love and understanding through this horror. He has to know we grieve with him and know that he will be a wonderful dad.

I realized this week I have lost my identity: part of my motherhood, my job as an RN due to my own illness, and my home! All in one year. No wonder I cry every day. I wake each morning not because I want to but my body is ready, not my mind!

My first thoughts are of Toni. Why can't I get the thought of my child with a gun in her mouth. It nauseates me. It's two years now and it is like yesterday. My chest and arms are squeezing in pain when I cry (there is a connection of the heart to the hands!)

Second thoughts: my grand daughter. She'll never know how much her mom loved her, taught her in the four short years they had together and all she still had left to teach her.

Third: I might as well get up so this day will be over! I must live for the living, and yet to be born. I must find my purpose, my lesson of this lifetime: but it hurts so much!

IT'S THE REALITY I MUST FACE.

INTRODUCTION

There are many people who are diagnosed with bipolar disease. Personally I believe we are all bipolar in a sense. It just depends how far the pendulum swings! We all have good days, bad days and horrible days. It's how we handle these moods and deal with them becomes the decisive factor! Most people who are diagnosed 'bipolar' are intelligent and deceitful.

WHY? THE STIGMA!

They become the Masters of Disguise! They can hide their illness until the pendulum loses balance. Signs are subtle and have to be paid attention to before the balance is lost. Treatment is paramount. We have learned through research that a steady routine, proper diet and exercise can help keep the balance, but sometimes medication needs to be introduced into the mix. Now there lies the problem. It may not take the first medication ordered to work and it may take weeks to recognize this. Another medication again may not work. Again another few weeks lost. This is not exclusive to mental illness. We all have different metabolism and what works for one person may not work for another, i.e. : the first cardiac drug a doctor orders may not be the one for a particular patient, but usually that is picked up quicker. This trial and error is very frustrating for the bipolar individual as the high is so invigorating, they would rather not give it up. Unfortunately the lows can lead to suicide. It's frustrating for the patient and the loved ones as well, just as any disease effects all loved ones. I cry not only for my family's loss but for all those that have lost a loved one in a tragedy: whether from suicide, sudden death, or from the horrors of war. Loosing a loved one and not being able to say goodbye is unbearable. We especially should treat our armed forces who have suffered mental and physical harm with dignity and treat them royally!

3/26/2015

This particular day the co pilot of Airbus A320 deliberately crashed his plane into the Alps taking not only his life, but 149 innocent people with him. The stigma of his illness and its implications on his career prevented him from sharing his illness. This alone shows how we need to educate and stop the stigma. My heart breaks for all those families that lost their loved ones and to the copilot's family as well. In such an educated society we still have so much to learn. Had he gone to his superiors, maybe he could have taken a medical leave, gotten help. There's also the case recently of a diagnosed schizophrenic man that was killed by the police within minutes of arriving at his home. His mother asked for a trained police assistance explaining the situation. There is training for police called CIT (crisis intervention training) which police receive initially but do not have to maintain updates. This is a crucial problem as research improves our understanding and reaction to illness. In nursing, every nurse has to retake certain courses (required to work) to keep updated with new treatments, drugs, etc. BLS (basic life support) and ACLS (advanced cardiac life support), crucial for updates for nurses and doctors alike.

New drugs and studies show and change how we deal with certain illness', especially cardiac arrest. We ignore mental health until there is a crisis or it hits home. It hit my home and family like a tornado! As humans we forget too quickly and move on to the next BIG story or crisis, thanks to media intervention and repetition. Killings in theaters, ISIS: the news keeps us well informed and we forget our focus.

USA Article 12/26/2014

ACCORDING TO THE NATIONAL INSTITUTE OF AMERICANS

With mental health, neglect of Americans with serious mental illness costs the nation $444 billion a year, mostly from lost earnings- and consigns millions to lives of suffering, addiction, homelessness or incarceration. Unfortunately suicide rates are on the rise and the victims are getting younger and younger. According to the books and research I've done, once someone decides to take their life, you can't stop them. It is a spur of the moment decision, irrational and not intended to hurt anyone but themselves to relieve themselves of their torment. Their thinking is irrational, which makes it too difficult to understand and wrap our head around it.

I hope the latest incidents do not increase the stigma but play a role in eliminating it and educating people that there is hope and help. Is one embarrassed to tell someone they have thyroid disease? Diabetes? NO, it's a chemical imbalance! Isn't this what mental illness is? There is constant research in this field which is lacking financial support. MRI's and blood tests may shed light on mental disorders.

CHAPTER 1

I used to wake with a song in my head. NOT ANYMORE! Now tears flowing down my cheeks.

The worst day of my life I was 13 and my boyfriend and I broke up. We would get back together year after year and finally married May 3, 1974.

After all I knew he was my soul mate: it was the best day of my life. Our first anniversary I spent alone, we separated: the worst day of my life. Of course as usual we got back together. We had the best day of our lives on August 21, 1977 when we gave birth to a beautiful perfect girl: Toni Anne. She was such a joy and so smart! She could sing all the songs from the show Annie at age two, Tomorrow being her favorite.

Another best day: September 7, 1981. Another beautiful baby girl: Dana Jeanne. Precocious and smart of course. We were a happy family, tired of NY winters and moved to Florida. I was seven months pregnant and beaming. May 19, 1983, another best day of our lives: Michael Angelo was born. Cute as a button and followed his sisters around everywhere once he started walking.

Toni was a second mother to her siblings. She read to them at night, put on plays, bossed them around and of course had the usual sibling fights. Life was never easy, but we managed. I had to work so we could make ends meet and do fun things with the children. So many happy days: birthdays, holidays, graduations, award ceremonies, tee ball, cheer leading, dance lessons. We were involved parents.

Twenty years of ups and downs, parents sick/dying, but we survived till the worst day of my life We divorced. My husband was diagnosed bipolar and it became impossible to stay married as he wouldn't seek treatment. My soul mate and I were through, there was no talking to him. I worked in ICU as an RN and changed from night shift to day shift. Toni was in High School, Dana in Middle School and Michael had just turned ten years old.

Struggled being a single mom but things got better. I had three beautiful children still giving me "best days". I changed jobs to work in the Recovery Room which enabled me to make extra money being 'on call", besides I couldn't work nights anymore and leave my children alone. I wanted my children to go to private school and get the best education I could afford.

Toni went to University of Florida, received her masters in accounting and then went to Florida State, graduating third in her law class. She married her college sweetheart (also studying law at FSU) and was a stunning bride. I was hoping it was one of the best days of her life! It became one for me.

Dana went to University of Central Florida and graduated with her BS in art. She got her first job in an art gallery on Worth Ave. She was in love and she and Nelson made a perfect couple.

Michael went to FSU, enrolled in a special hospitality program for golfers. His first year of college he starting acting erratic. Toni was living in Tallahassee and was giving me reports of his behavior. I was doing a travel nurse assignment in Orlando and drove like I was in the INDY 500 to Tallahassee. He was diagnosed bipolar (genetics). He was admitted to the hospital for a week. My baby boy: worst day of my life. He has since realized after therapy, drugs, and good nutrition, rest and exercise keeps him on track and he's doing great.

I moved, made new friends at my new job in a small county hospital, of course in the Recovery Room (known as PACU now: post anesthesia care unit). I made more new friends at jazzercise and was content with my new home and new job.

On December 31, 2008 my first grandchild, a girl, was born and it was another best day. I would make frequent 6 hour drives to Tallahassee to be with Toni, my son in law and my grand-daughter. Happy Days.

Michael moved to California and soon after Dana and Nelson also moved there. I wasn't happy about the distance, but we had a wonderful relationship and after all I moved away from my family and encouraged my children to follow their dreams and their hearts.

AUGUST 5, 2013

THE WORST DAY OF MY LIFE

It will forever be! Every day is August 5th now. My precious child, my Toni, took her life! How is this possible? I wake with tears, I sleep with tears. I ask her every night to visit me in a dream. I pray to God and all my deceased loved ones to look after her. I ask her to send signs to her daughter in dreams.

I tear with a word, a song, a memory, a smell. She was diagnosed bipolar but didn't like the medications nor the stigma.   She became a MASTER OF DISGUISE.

I struggle with denial every day, every minute. People say it will never get better but easier: BULLSHIT!

I read a lot, try to keep busy, wear a mask myself when I'm with people. She's always on my mind. I cry alone, in pain and disbelief even now although it is 2 years. As I am typing this, her birthday is in 2 days. Writing this has been a catharsis for me but this week has been unbearably painful. I am not alone in this pain, talking to Dana and Michael this week we all feel the pain, it's palpable!

Michael and Dana both married in 2014 and the elephant in the room was with me through their happiness, and my happiness for them. They suffer so much, too, and we talk a lot about how our lives have changed. The 'NEW NORMAL', so it is called. This is anything but normal!

CHAPTER 2

POEMS AND QUOTES

"THE REALITY IS THAT YOU WILL GRIEVE FOREVER. YOU WILL NOT 'GET OVER' THE LOSS OF A LOVED ONE; YOU WILL LEARN TO LIVE WITH IT. YOU WILL HEAL AND YOU WILL REBUILD YOURSELF AROUND THE LOSS YOU HAVE SUFFERED. YOU WILL BE WHOLE AGAIN BUT YOU WILL NEVER BE THE SAME. NOR SHOULD YOU WANT TO.

Elisabeth Kubler Ross

THE WORST PRISON IS THE DEATH OF ONE'S CHILD; YOU NEVER GET OUT OF IT, (quote from movie) 'I LOVED YOU SO LONG'.

This has been the year of WTF happened. You can't make this shit up! I have left names out to protect and be respectful of those I know would want it that way. I found these poems I had written at the time of my daughters death.

I stare into space hoping to see your face

I nursed and watched you grow from

breast milk to cheerios

You couldn't fight your demons and left us all too soon

I pray you are at peace now

Yet my life is ruined

Happy moments shared is all I have

I'd rather hold you tight

Instead I think

THIS ISN'T RIGHT

They say life goes on

We must struggle through the "new"

I love you so

Of that you surely knew

Always in my heart

We'll never be apart

I am not alone, but yet I am

My hurt is mine, yours is yours

compare them not

Part of me is missing

I'm no longer whole

Two thirds is hanging on

You took with you my soul

My day starts by missing you

By night time I am numb

You left a hole in many hearts

How can we let you go?

I'm shattered and confused

My strength has all been used

I long to hold you near

That is my only prayer

A parents deepest wish

Is never go through this

So many questions to ask

Yet everyday I wear a mask

Poem written 13 months later. Nothing has changed.

Tears express the pain

There really is no gain

My heart is full of rain

The thunderstorm is strong

I hear it in a song

I feel it with a smell

Words a living hell

A smile, a picture, a phrase

I want you back in my days

There never will be a drought

Of that there is no doubt

I truly hope you found peace

My life is filled with grief

CHAPTER 3

THE NIGHTMARE BEGINS

I don't remember how I spent the rest of the night after screaming and banging the walls. I called, Dana, Michael, my ex husband, my sister and a friend who came over immediately with her husband. Everyone else I called was so far away. The rest of the night remains a blur.

I don't remember how Dana got to Florida, but she drove up to Tallahassee (I couldn't drive or think straight). My sister and brother-in-law came to Tallahassee and again how they got there and back to NJ is still a mystery to me. The wake was a nightmare yet I couldn't cry. THIS IS NOT HAPPENING! I never worried about her doing something like this. She had a good career, a good husband, a beautiful daughter and a lovely home. I did hate the fact that there were guns in the house, and they were well aware of my feelings.

My son-in-law said he was going to change the safe combination that morning and he told her he was taking her to the hospital. Obviously he realized the situation was beyond his control. Something triggered her response and none of us will ever know. SO MUCH HURT!

AUGUST 21,2013

Toni would have been 36 y.o. Dana, myself and two of Toni's friends set off balloons at a lake. My son-in-law didn't think it would be good for my grand-daughter. She needs to grieve, yet she's so young and doesn't understand the finality of death. I know he wants to keep her safe and happy. Eventually as she gets older there will be so many unanswered questions. My family intends to make sure she gets the support she needs.

I just kept saying "why can't I cry"! Denial. Shock. We found out 6 months later it was more than just shock and denial.

SEPT 1, 2013

I wake each morning feeling someone kicked me in my gut. I don't want this reality. How could she do this? I don't know when the numbness will go away. I don't give a shit about anything, everything is trivial after this!

SEPT 2, 2013

My son-in laws birthday. Everything so close and so unbearable. I sent him a copy of the book, 'Finding Peace Without All the Pieces', by LaRita Archibald to him. I do cry but I know it's not a guttural cry like when my parents died. Something was very wrong. My eyes feel dry and crying just confirms the reality, not the acceptance. Each morning is worse. The nightmare isn't going away.

I planned a trip to California to be with Dana and Michael (on short term disability). We needed family comfort as we were and still are suffering so much.

SEPT 4, 2013

Therapist feels I'm on the right track for healing. What a crooked, winding track it is! Grieving suicide pulls all your emotions together like a ball of twine which unravels slowly, constantly getting knotted.

I got in touch with NAMI (National Alliance for Mental Illness). I had contact with them when my ex-husband was diagnosed and again when Michael was diagnosed his first year at college. Michael trusted me, saw a therapist and took his meds. He had to change his major but he persevered.

I signed up and formed a team to walk for NAMI of Broward 'TEARS FOR TONI'. We collected around $2000 for mental health research. It is not decreasing in the cause of death, but increasing! So many diseases are caused by stress, yet we give mental illness the least amount of research. Our society has to be educated about mental illness and deal with it like we do with all diseases. There should be no stigma: it's a chemical imbalance!

I went to a grief sharing meeting. Not for me, not for everyone. I'm a doer. To feel better I have to make someone else feel better. I guess all the years of nursing ingrained that in me. I spoke with my friend Jan who lost a son to suicide, which was helpful. It's a bond you wish you never have to share. People say "I can't imagine how you feel"! NO, YOU CAN'T, and I hope you never will.

SEPT 7,2013

Dana's birthday. Another tough day to endure. Toni was always the first to send a card. They were beyond sisters, they were friends and rivals as most siblings are.

I woke with the song, 'The Sun Will Come Out Tomorrow', whispering in my ear. I know Toni put it there. She sang that since she was two years old. She loved the movie, 'ANNIE'. We took her to see the Broadway show before we moved to Florida.

This morning my tremors are bad, my gut and heart are aching. Spoke with my son-in-law over an hour last night. We are both tormented by the "should haves and if's"! He told me Toni had told him four years ago she was going to commit suicide. She told him how and where: outside the house so she wouldn't dirty the house! WTF: how do you ignore that. How do you not tell me, her mother, knowing the family history? Was it post partum depression? Were these remarks forgotten in the everyday living, working, taking care of a child? She really couldn't have meant it. I believe the majority of people have suicidal thoughts at one time or another during lifes stresses. She was always top in her class. Class president all 4 years of high school, graduated with her masters in accounting from the University of Florida, graduated third from Florida State law school and had a great job with a prestigious law firm in Tallahassee!

My grand-daughter asked her dad " what happened to mommy? We were watching Mickey Mouse, she went outside and never came back?" He told her Toni fell off a ladder. Breaking my heart, how does it still beat?

Every day the pain and sorrow surmount, it's so painful. I grab the phone to call someone but hang up instead. I want to call her! Everyone says to call them anytime. I can't. No one can make this go away or make it better, there are no words. Some tears need to be shed alone.

My friend Terri comes and just listens, sometimes we don't even talk, but it's comforting. My best friend Karen moves to Ohio, but she is always a comfort to me, always there for me, she was Toni's godmother on her confirmation. She is my soul sister!

I was supposed to die first, every parent knows that. I was getting organized with the Neptune Society before this tragedy. Toni told me she thought that was morbid. I wasn't getting any younger and I didn't want to have my death be a burden for my children. What she did was beyond morbid! HOW? WHY?

I cry for my grand-daughter because she will never know her sweet beautiful mother who loved her so much. How much will she remember? Will she remember her mom getting in the crib with her to get her to fall asleep? Sleeping on the floor for hours because she couldn't fall asleep. How much both will miss. It is slowly eviscerating my being.

SEPT 11, 2013

A somber day in America. Waking up sucks. I'm shaking more than usual. Side effects from antidepressant? Am I shaking on purpose? Just what the hell is going on, yet I still am not mourning as I feel I should, still in denial, still numb.

Toni told me once, "I can't look my daughter in the face, I let her down."

Of course I responded, "You're a great mom, look at the role model you had!"

She always had to strive to be superior, go above and beyond. She wanted to be the best and didn't realize she already was!

My anger persists. Why didn't she confide in me? She always had in the past. I respected her request not to drive to Tallahassee and will forever regret it. How can I go back to work when the mornings are so unbearable? I do a lot of reading on grief and mental disorders. I have to constantly be busy.

My friends and family are supportive that I, Dana and Michael will keep Toni's spirit alive for her daughter. We have agreed we will make it our mission to always be there for her, for Toni!

Again this morning, "The sun will come out tomorrow," she is with me! I have some of her ashes, I believe I have her heart, yet it saddens me to think of my child as ashes. It's incomprehensible and haunting.

It's amazing when you open up to people, especially when something like suicide smacks you in the face, you learn about other peoples dealings with suicide even though you knew them for years, but never knew. Everyone knew why I wasn't at work, everyone was supportive , not only emotionally, monetary as well. The doctors, nurses, techs, even our volunteers collected money which I donated to NAMI.

I'll never understand how she was able to do it. My, son said, "Mom, her soul left her days before." That was such a comfort to me. I went to California for a week. I needed my children and they needed me. Dana and Michael are my rocks. I know I worry them, I zone out, I walk hunched over.

Dana and I went wedding dress shopping. Of course we talked about Toni. Dana was going to send her an official invitation to be her maid of honor. She hadn't sent it yet, another 'what if'?

Nelson and Dana took me for a ride to Joshua Tree National Park where they were planning to have their wedding. I had seen a lot of California with Michael since he moved there first and we had a wonderful mother/son bonding trip to Sequoia State Park. I digress.

SEPT 27, 2013

Back from California, withdrawal from my children. I want my body to implode. The days are getting harder, reality sucks. I made an appointment with a medium. I really felt I was with Toni that night. Dana was upset since she is friends with the Amazing Randi who exposed charlatans. My medium was also my acupuncturist, I was having severe neck and back pain. Mary was healing me spiritually, she wasn't curing me, just helping me as a therapist. I always felt comforted after being with her. I can't stop shaking!

OCTOBER 4-7, 2013

Spent the weekend with my son-in-law and grand-daughter. I can't believe two months have passed. It is too difficult being in the house that started my daughters downward spiral. Being in the kitchen, using her utensils, I can't handle it. They were supposed to sign the contract on the new house the day of her funeral. Am I more angry at myself for not realizing my child was so distraught or that she didn't confide in me? Distance muffles a lot. My son-in-law shared some disturbing thoughts. First time we really had a heart to heart talk. How do we get through this? Of course I cried all the way home, all 6 hours from Tallahassee to Palm City, Florida.

I went to a family NAMI meeting when I returned home. Everyone keeps reinforcing I'm on the right track. I'm not curled up in bed, sleeping all the time, instead I am constantly having to do something to keep going, stop thinking. I read in one of many books about grief: loosing a spouse is like loosing an arm, loosing a child is like loosing a lung. I keep praying I'm in a coma, going to wake up and this is all a horrible nightmare.

OCTOBER 10-30, 2013

I returned to work. My manager and charge nurse

were so supportive, even when I'd forget to show up for work, or came in late! I was given a lot of slack but did my job as usual, keeping busy and concentrating on my patients problems not mine. It definitely was therapeutic.

I am not religious although I was brought up Catholic. I am spiritual and feel my beliefs are personal. I did a lot of soul searching.

It nauseates me to think of my child with a gun in her mouth, yet I can't get that visual out of my mind, which makes me feel out of my mind!

Statistics state that more deaths from guns are suicides not murders! If there is a gun available, a suicidal person will use it   October 26th was the California AFSP (American foundation for suicide prevention) walk. Dana and Michael formed a team and collected a lot of donations to the cause. I couldn't be more proud. They are proactive. They are my reason for living.

Dana, Nelson, Michael and Melissa came to Florida for Christmas. My son-in-law and grand-daughter came too. We had a decent holiday, but we all felt the loss. We even had a birthday party for my grand-daughter.

JANUARY 2014

The month of January I returned to work: 12 hour shifts, call one day a week and every 6th weekend. I was getting slower and slower at work. I was having trouble starting IV's which I was the "go to" person before. I had been through so many changes in all my nursing years I knew eventually I would get back to my nursing expertise in time. My manager and charge nurse put up with me because they knew I needed time to adjust to the loss of my daughter and I had an excellent track record.

Unfortunately my manager and charge nurse moved to a satellite hospital and the new manager and charge nurse were, besides not being qualified for their jobs, were not as compassionate, they didn't know the real Denise.

Back to my medium encounter. Mary had her two sisters, whom I had never met and were also mediums. One sister kept seeing a young child dancing and singing; that was my Toni for sure. They said Toni admitted to having delusions as a child. My son in law actually informed me she told him that once!

Through the medium Toni apologized for being fresh

at times and for not telling me enough how much she loves me.

She related she had to end it that way because she didn't want her daughter growing up with a crazy mother and asked me to nurture her daughter like I did her. She also told me to tell her husband to FUCK OFF if he gives me resistance!

According to 'MANY LIVES, MANY MASTERS' by Dr. Brian Weiss, we come back to learn how to be truly spiritual beings. Whose lesson was this? Mine?, Her husbands?, Her daughter or siblings? I am trying so hard to dig into my inner core and find my purpose. I'm thinking it may be this story, my catharsis and hopefully an insight even if just for one person.

I had an appointment for a head CT ordered by my primary doctor since I complained of tiredness, missing work, being forgetful and having headaches. I knew my personality was dull, not my usual self. My daughter died, but let's be cautious.

FEB 6, 2014

I returned home from my CT having a cup of coffee and cereal when I got a call from my primary doctors office telling me to go straight to the ER, do not drive myself: THIS IS NOT GOOD (even a non medical person could figure that out!) There were so many symptoms, I along with my fellow medical professionals I worked with blamed on depression, besides I am the care giver!

A huge tumor was sitting on my frontal lobe, suppressing my emotions (hence why I couldn't cry, why my personality was changing, why I was slowing down at work. I wasn't me!)

I wasn't fazed by this. Emotionless I sat in the ER eating a turkey sandwich while my friend Terri cried. How do I tell my children this six months after their sister passed? I was supposed to go to California for Melissa's bridal shower, had my ticket to leave in 2 days. NOT HAPPENING.

Thank God for friends. Marilyn and Terri stayed with me 12 hours in the ER. Somehow my friend Patty got Virgin America to give my ticket to my daughter Dana so she could come to Florida and cancelled my flight to California. I wasn't allowed to drive and was scheduled for surgery the following week.

I never had a seizure which amazed everyone, considering the size of the tumor. My surgeon told me it was the size of his fist and he was a big man!

I named my tumor Penni. My mother wanted to name me Penni so I figured that's where she landed. Anything I couldn't do I would blame on Penni.

FEB 13, 2014

I quit smoking the morning of surgery. I knew my anesthesiologist (perk of being a PACU nurse) and immediately felt reassured with my surgeon. Dana and Michael were at my side pre op, even my ex husband came. I know Toni was there. The Anesthesiologist held my fingerprint necklace for me during the case.

I wanted my sister there, she was stuck in Puerto Rico, but she didn't come even though she couldn't get back to NJ because of the weather. I'm still having a difficult time dealing with the hurt. A six hour craniotomy is not like an appendectomy, although any surgery can turn into a disaster. Brain and heart surgeries are pretty much the most intricate and dangerous. Being a nurse I was thankful that my frontal lobe was impaired. I wasn't afraid. I trusted my staff and I just knew that I would either stay with Dana and Michael or be with Toni and my parents. It was in God's hands.

My fear of death dissipated. I really didn't fear death in the past just how I would die. I had seen too much unnecessary suffering at work. We are kinder to animals than people!

I woke up the next day in ICU. Not a pretty site, I'm sure. I was extubated because I was breathing on my own. The first words I spoke were, "This is fucking insanity." I was on the wrong side of the bed! Everyone was thrilled the old Denise was back. No more Penni, does that make me Penniless?

FEB 17-MARCH 10, 2014

During this time I had physical therapy at home, home nursing visits and a medication regime daily! Dana stayed with me and I recovered quickly and positively. My tumor was non cancerous. I returned to work three weeks after surgery. I had little time left of my short term disability and the new manager was getting ready to post my position, never expecting me to bounce back so quickly. The new staff finally met the real Denise RN., competent, quick and efficient, not to mention dependable. They had only known Penni!

MARCH 2014

During this time I actually grieved my daughters death and am still grieving. I cry a lot. I spent many hours writing letters to numerous people. I wanted to get more involved with NAMI, now that I had motivation. I wrote about the need for better mental care to President Obama, Ellen Degeneres, Robin Roberts, Whoopie Goldberg, Governor Scott, Marco Rubio and Patrick Murphy. The only personal letter I received back was from the White House. I wonder if any of the others even saw my letters. I expressed concern that it takes someone famous to bring light to mental health needs. Shortly after, Robin Williams took his own life. At this time I was also having issues with my mortgage since I had to retire early. I also wrote to OSHA, the CDC, and Erin Brockovich. Of course I notified Human Resources that I was the fourth nurse in this small, six bed PACU to develop a brain tumor! I have found more incidences since then and wonder how many people may have moved from this area and not realize the 'coincidence'. I can only pursue one issue at a time and have devoted most of my time to mental health issues and educating the media through NAMI.

I started this 2 years ago, and now with all these

random theater killing, ISIS, plane incidences and school shootings I feel the need even more so for educating the media. It's all about STIGMA, not about treatment!

CHAPTER 4

LIFE GOES ON

APRIL 11, 2014

My son Michael married a beautiful woman Melissa. She is not only lovely physically but has a beautiful soul. It was a fabulous wedding even with the elephant in the room. Michael became known as 'groomzilla'. Melissa was checking the hotel list and someone had circled Michael's name and wrote "high maintenance!"

Their first dance, which was actually there dances were a joy to watch. Of course Michael imitated Michael Jackson, something he had been doing as a child. All my children were animated and loved entertaining. He arranged a flash dance through the internet so all the guests were part of the celebration and it was a blast. He had a special table set up in memory of Toni, but I'm sure she was with us in spirit. My son-in-law and grand-daughter didn't come which upset Michael since he is so family oriented and wanted part of his sister there.

MAY 21, 2014

I went for one cyber knife treatment per the guidance of my neurosurgeon. He said there was one area he didn't excise because it was too vascular. I asked if it was possible I could stroke and he assured me not. I did go to dinner with friends the same night and I felt fine.

MAY 22, 2014

I was at work, just discharging a patient from the recovery room and noticed my left arm and leg getting numb. I had expressive aphasia (difficulty speaking), signs of a stroke! Of course the staff put me in a wheelchair and brought me straight to the ER. I was transferred to our sister hospital ICU since we had no neurology unit. My medications were adjusted and I was acting like a real asshole. There is only one patient worse than a nurse and that's a doctor! I didn't have a stroke. My symptoms were diagnosed as simple complex seizures, probably due to swelling.

My atypical seizures started with ringing in my left ear while it was jiggling and feeling like it was going to fall off my head. My left foot numbness progressed up my leg. The pounding in my ear was loud and obnoxious, like someone banging on an anvil. I would think people were talking or crying when they weren't. The episodes were less frequent so I was discharged with a new medication regime. Being a seasoned nurse I made an old fashioned medication sheets and would mark off as I took my meds. I set my iPhone timer on to remind me to take my meds as the medications were making me more forgetful than the tumor did.

After discharge my dear friend Terri (ICU Neuro RN) was my on call nurse. I seemed to be doing better and was totally aware of what my symptoms were, and would be in tune if they became worse. (Nursing Bravado!)

MEMORIAL DAY WEEKEND 2014

Had bad night because of the banging in my ear. Terri stayed overnight. I finally woke her up and asked her to take me to the hospital: "I'm going to die today". She cried and I consoled her! I was ready, I was still depressed about Toni and was ready to meet her. We spoke to the PA on the phone, who of course told me to go to the ER. again my medications were adjusted. I didn't die.

I was referred to an ENT doctor and was told I had

'palatal myoclonus': constant clicking of the soft palate, so he added Flexiril to my medical regimen. It did nothing! My primary doctor started me on Klonipin and it seemed to work immediately. No more voices, no more banging!

PROBLEM: I was informed I had no more time off from work with pay.

DECISION: I had been working 43 years as a nurse, close to retirement so I applied for Social Security Disability, which my primary doctor had been encouraging me to do all along. I no longer felt I would be efficient as a nurse. I didn't want to jeopardize anyone's health.

I already started proceedings for a loan modification, but after tons of paper work, was denied. I was going on Social Security, making half of what I was making as a nurse monthly. This wasn't going to work. My world was falling apart. My child is dead. WTF is happening?

I was crying on a regular basis for Toni, but able to function at home with cooking and cleaning, although sometimes I would forget I was cooking or I would forget to put the oven on. I would become distracted easily and start 2-3 projects at a time. I was O.C.D.

34

and A.D.D.!

The only show I could watch on TV was 'THE BIG BANG THEORY' and the only music I could listen to was Jason Mraz.

Fortunately, this was considered a different event so I was able to collect short term disability again till August 21st (Toni's birthday). So after careful thought, I decided to quit my job on August 5th and find another job part time. BEST LAID PLANS!

JUNE 6, 2014

Last night I stared at Toni's picture and for the first time saw pain in her eyes. Am I going crazy or is she sending me a message? Sometimes I feel the only way to get through this is to believe she is really alive somewhere. It's too painful to cry, my whole body hurts. I want to wake up and it's July 2012!

JUNE/JULY 2014

I spent many hours dyeing coffee filters peach for my darling daughter Dana's wedding. She wanted to decorate her wedding venue with something she saw on Pinterest. I dyed 10,000 coffee filters. Being on steroids it was easy and it kept me busy, that and more loan modification paperwork.

I invited my son-in-law and grand-daughter to the Weeki Watchee Mermaid show. We met on the west coast of Florida and my grand-daughter loved it. We had a pleasant weekend. I treated for dinner and breakfast since it was fathers day. I gave my son-in-law a case of paper towels which he loved (OCD) and some of Toni's things for my grand-daughter.

AUGUST 21, 2014

Toni would have been 37 today. She will be forever young, forever in my heart. Dana came from California since her bridesmaids paid for her trip so we could have a bridal shower for her.

That night we went to the beach and were going to let off lanterns for Toni but it was too windy. A couple I met at a support group came: Betz and Troy. After tw0 deployments to Iraq their son came home and committed suicide July 4, 2013. There unfortunately is a special bond among families that have endured suicide, especially of a child. They bought balloons with lights in them. Many of my friends came. Dana's future in laws came. We all said something about our loss. It was a beautiful, sad event.

AUGUST 23,2014

Bridal shower for Dana. All Dana's friends, my friends and her future in-laws contributed to the event. I made a slide show for Dana as I did for Toni. Dana didn't want any wedding bells decor so of course I painted huge wedding bells on my glass sliding doors and hung streamers of wedding bells from the ceiling. Even though it was a happy occasion, there was sadness underlying it all. No maid of honor, just an elephant.

I dream a lot, but usually can't remember them but I always know when I wake if I was with Toni. One dream, a beautiful dream I do remember and will never forget as it was so wonderfully sad.: I was packing to go to Tallahassee, and Toni told me not to come. She said: " It has to be this way" She gave me a big hug with her wings and kissed me, said she loves me and she will keep sending me signs.

Was that my chance to say goodbye? It hurt so bad and of course I woke crying. At times I swear I hear her voice. I'll believe what I want, what makes me smile in the face of this tragedy. I find pennies in the oddest places. I moved into an apartment which was empty yet there was a penny on the counter. I know she is with me, it's her sign. I have a jar I fill up every time I find a penny!

If you look for signs you will find them: BELIEVE.

SEPT 11, 2014

I was going to call Toni today to tell her how late I slept. I usually wake up early. Michael had bought her a magnet of the World Trade Center when we went to NY. I sent it to my grand-daughter for Christmas. GOD, HOW I MISS HER.

I never went out today. I spent the day writing letters to my grand-daughter hoping I can paint an accurate picture of the wonderful mother she was, how much she loved her and that I know she is looking after her.

SEPT 16, 2014

I woke at 4:30. I wasn't angry, just confused. I'm trying to understand why my son-in-law still has guns in the house. Everything I read says that nothing or no one can stop a person from completing the task one feels has to be done to stop the pain and torment. This story is about the stigma of mental illness and the hardships people endure. This is about hope that someone will get some insight, inspiration. Even if only one life is saved it will be worth it. If one parent finds strength it will be worth it. Read the suggested readings. Look up the references. Just knowing there is help, helps.

Toni needed to be hospitalized, all beyond my son-in-laws and his parents capabilities of understanding. They tried their best, but I will never understand why they didn't let me know how serious the situation had become. That knew I dealt with it before and have a medical background. Why didn't I recognize the control and denial issue: my GUILT!

SEPT 21, 2014

I applied for Social Security since I thought my 'ear episodes' were over and I wanted the option to work. Keep busy, feel useful. I'm 64 today. I will never get another card from Toni. I put up the last birthday and mothers day cards she sent me. I have in my bedside drawer letters from her while she was in college. I still don't have the courage to read them.

SEPT 22, 2014

I woke this morning with "MY FUNNY VALENTINE" whispering in my ear. I would sing that to her in the car when I took her to my mothers.

My mother watched her while I went to work. I would sing and she would eat her pretzels and cheerios while reading her plastic books. They kept her busy and happy in the car. Imagine no DVDs! Just her and I singing and enjoying the ride and each other.

CHAPTER 5

SEPT 27- 0CT 7, 2014

I left for California for Dana and Nelsons wedding on 9/27. I awoke at 5:55, the time Toni was born: she was coming with me! Dana bought a flower girl dress and desert boots for my grand-daughter since the wedding was going to be in the desert in Joshua Tree. We were all so happy my son-in-law and grand-daughter were coming, since they missed Michael and Melissa's wedding.

Dana was an exquisite bride, radiating joy and love. Everything was wonderful and I know Toni was there with us. It was wonderful getting there before the big day so we could spend time together flower shopping, putting bouquets together, getting mani's and pedi's. Enjoying the moments, making the memories. It was different than your traditional wedding, but fantastic and unique like Dana and Nelson, so fitting. They beamed with love which spread to all the guests. The weather was perfect, the scenery incredible, the bride and groom were perfect, just like Michael and Melissa!

Even in the desert we had wedding crashers. Dana and Nelson like Michael and Melissa put a separate spot with a dedication to lost loved ones.

Returning home always leaves an emptiness, a sadness in your heart. Both my children lived in California and Toni was in heaven. It's wonderful to have good friends. When you move away from your core family, your friends become your family. I have been very lucky in that respect. Everyone can sympathize with you, but can never really know how deep the wound is after a suicide. It's unimaginable with such a cacophony of emotions.

I am so happy Dana and Michael found wonderful caring partners. They have not only helped them endure the loss of their sibling, but have been a great support with love and kindness through this tragedy.

OCTOBER 8-20, 2014

The wedding was October 4th and now back home, after being denied loan modification I had to put my home up for short sale. The problem is you can't get help until you stop paying your mortgage, then they get interested in helping you. I tried all the right ways and got denial after denial. Somehow they had me making more money not working than working!

Then they told me I was eligible for a Florida Hardest hit Program: more beuraCRAPTIC bullshit.

I wrote to the CEO of the bank and they said they would try to work out my loan modification yet again. The only positive about all this it had me distracted at times from my real problem: MY CHILD IS DEAD, I've lost part of my head, and now I'm loosing my home. WTF is all I can say. I don't know myself how I continue to function. For Dana and Michael I must be strong but I wonder why I'm still alive since my heart is fractured. I pray to Mary as she also lost a child, she suffered, I suffer.

I know I dreamed about Toni last night, but can't remember the dream. It happens all so often. I was reading "THE WHEEL OF LIFE" by Elisabeth Kubler Ross. It lifted my spirits. I've always admired her work. She became popular when I first started nursing. I was intrigued with her philosophy and was fortunate enough to attend one of her lectures.

CHAPTER 6

I suggested to my son-in-law we meet in St. Augustine for thanksgiving. He told me he was invited to a girls house whom he had been "talking to". Will I ever have another holiday with my grand-daughter? Other people have gone through this, I'm sure there are civil ways to work things out. I realize my grand-daughter needs a female role model, but it hurt to have my daughter semi-replaced so soon.

As I was writing this I realized my parents didn't have holidays and birthdays with my children. We chose to move away, which as I get older I regret.. Another what if we stayed in New York. When my parents came to Florida we had wonderful times. We played games, my dad played the piano, the children sang and put on plays for them. Our joy of being with them spilled over to our children and they cherished those moments. Our children were also lucky enough to have their paternal grandmother, aunt and cousins living in the same town, not to mention our close friends Terry(a different Terry) and Louie who lived three doors from us with their children, the same age as ours. We knew them from NY.

I cry for Toni and all she is missing with her daughter. I know she would have given Toni as much joy as Toni gave me. Dana and Michael miss her so much, and thankfully they do fill some of the void.

Her husband not only had a clue, she told him four years prior how and where she was going to kill herself: outside the house, so she wouldn't get the house dirty! I learned this postmortem. Did he attribute this to post partem depression? Whatever the case, when someone mentions, even lightly about suicide, don't ignore or pass it off, be on your guard! Bipolar suicide happens during the depression stage.

She seemed her usual self after the anxiety of childbirth and being a new mom. It's difficult to see signs through a phone conversation. Even when we would Skype, she seemed fine. She told me she was anxious so I encouraged her to seek professional help since we were both well aware of our family genetic history.

Ignorance and denial are the biggest problem when dealing with mental health issues, especially dealing with intelligent people. That's why it's so easy for them to become masters of disguise. She didn't want to take medication. Of course, being a nurse I would retaliate " I'm glad you're not a diabetic. It's all about the STIGMA. She didn't like the trial and error part of taking drugs either. All these drugs take weeks to maintain an appropriate level for the individual so trial and errors can take months. Unfortunately, most have side effects of increased depression and suicidal thoughts..What's wrong with this picture? Lack of research.

I love my grand-daughter, my mini Toni, my blood connection. I maintain contact by sending letters and little gifts periodically. I have to hold on to my life line just as my son-in-law has to hold on to his. I see how he adores and adorns her with love and care. I know he wants the best for her and is doing his best to give her a happy healthy childhood. Amazingly my grand-daughter remembers a lot about her mom. Her memory is incredible, as was her moms. Whenever I couldn't remember something I knew if I called Toni she'd know the answer.

OCTOBER 20-27, 2014

Took a rode trip for a week with my friend Terry. We went to Savannah, GA, Durham,NC, Blairsville, GA and St. Augustine. I wanted to stop in Tallahassee but my son-in-law said they were busy. Despite the rejection, we had a wonderful time. It was so relaxing until the day before we were leaving to go home. I started getting ringing in my ears. No other symptoms thank God. Fortunately it lessened on it's own when I returned to Florida.

OCTOBER 30, 2014

I asked my son-in-law what they were doing for Halloween. Toni always made it a big deal, just like I did. I used to make their costumes, in fact one of my favorite picture of Toni she is dressed up as Peter Pan for Halloween when she was three years old.

My grand-daughter was going to be Doc Mc Stuffin and he was going to be a flying monkey from the Wizard of OZ. Kidding I suggested I fly over on my broom and be the witch!..He actually sent me a picture of himself, my grand-daughter and the girl he's been seeing. My grand-daughter actually was dressed as Dorothy and his girlfriend was going to be the witch. I cried and cried, even though I realize he's young and they both need a female in their lives.

I wanted to buy the video's Toni enjoyed as a child (classics like the Wizard of OZ) but I was told not to make everything a memorial, she needs her own childhood. Michael told me to save them for he has children; so clever and thoughtful, easing the pain.

NOVEMBER 2014

I did some Christmas shopping today and without thinking picked up three Christmas ornaments as usual. I always did things in threes. I didn't realize till I got to the car and then the tears flowed. Of course I sent the third to my son-in-law and granddaughter. I don't think I'll ever get used to the "new normal".

Still hearing nothing from Social Security concerning disability, my primary care insisted I get a lawyer and gave me a referral. I did call him and he thought there could be no way they should refuse me, but he will definitely help me out if they do, which of course they did.

Today is actually August 21, 2015, Toni's BD and I'm still waiting with the lawyer to hear back about my disability. The lawyer found out Social Security never contacted my primary doctor, nor my neurologist, only my neurosurgeon. Well the last time I saw my neurosurgeon was my post operative check up!

The five stages of dying as defined by Elisabeth Kugler-Ross are: denial, anger, bargaining, depression and acceptance. I have found with suicide you experience these emotions simultaneously with guilt and blame. Not only is it exhausting, it is heart wrenching. It's like a twine of yarn being unraveled slowly, especially when you reach a knot! I believe I mentioned that before but I tend to repeat myself a lot lately.

Dear Lord, you had the chance to take me. Six hours in surgery, so I have to believe I still must have a purpose. I used to feel so blessed that our family had no real tragedies; you just never know.

Working as a nurse in ICU and PACU I have seen how much suffering and pain the human body can tolerate. What we can't see (thanks to drugs) is the mental anguish, pain and suffering. Believe me, it's there. We see it in the family members, but there are few words to ease the mental pain.

We all have it in varying degrees and we all handle mental anguish differently. Some of us become introverted, some lash out, some retaliate. I need something positive to endure the worst year of my life. So I wrote my story to convey to "endures":

YOU ARE NOT ALONE, YOU ARE NOT CRAZY!

Every one heals at their own pace, some never do. There is no right or wrong way to grieve, it's whatever works for you.

There is help available. Find it, use it, embrace it because the truth remains the same. Your loved one is no longer with you physically but always with you spiritually. Once we accept this truth we can deal with the mundane task of living.

So the bottom line is EVERYDAY is August 5th to me. Everyday I cry. We go through the everyday motions of living and hope we find small threads of happiness. The medium told me to look for signs. Since I named my tumor Penni. I have been finding pennies in odd places, have had flowers bloom out of season, hear pertinent songs when I am crying. Even though I always saw one or two rabbits around Easter, this year they are everywhere. It seems like every holiday she shows me she is with me.

I am not a survivor, just a mom enduring the worst year of my life. I'm trying to convey to others that life is survivable even under the worst of circumstances. It's not to say I haven't had thoughts of joining Toni, but the thoughts reverse when I think of my children and maybe some more grand children. Maybe some happier days ahead. Hard to envision right now.

My hope is that by conveying my story, some eyes have been opened, some heads taken out of the sand. No one should have to suffer this tragedy. Pay attention to clues, they may be subtle but they are there. It has been researched that many intelligent people take their lives. They are so clever though that they mask the signs.

My good friend Marilyn bought a plaque for me:

YOU NEVER KNOW HOW STRONG YOU ARE UNTIL BEING STRONG IS THE ONLY CHOICE YOU HAVE!

I have it hanging among pictures of my darling Toni!

Another poem I wrote:

The feeling inside me will never leave

I wear it as my outer sleeve

some even call it grief

The threads are stitched so tight

They can't let in the slightest light

No one cal pull it apart

It's appliqued with all our hearts

That keep them from coming apart

Love and strength, forming a clot

I stay behind and wait

Till I can meet you at the gate

THROUGH TIME INTO HEALING
by BRIAN WEISS:

Many people have the same experiences and beliefs you do perhaps many more than you can imagine. And many of these people feel discouraged from communicating their experiences for the same reasons you do. Still others may be expressing them, but in private. It is important to keep an open mind, to trust your experiences. Don't let the dogma and beliefs of others undermine your personal experience and perception of reality.

LISA BELKIN QUOTE:

"When our spouse dies, we are widowed. When a child dies, we are speechless."

Toni will NEVER be dead to me! My heart aches with love for her all day and night. When a puzzle piece is missing there is no way to put it back together. There will always be a void, an empty space, a clogged artery no stent can replace.

I have learned to despise the word dead. She is not dead, she is alive in every memory I and everyone who knew her. Dead denotes finality, there is no finality for those of us left behind.

CHAPTER 7

MARCH 10, 2015

I finally spent time with my son-in-law and grand-daughter in St. Augustine. We had a wonderful time. We share so much pain. My grand-daughter calls me grandma genius (she couldn't pronounce Denise; love it!) I had her birthday presents and her Easter presents. I gave her a Disney calendar, it was something new to her. We wrote in everyone's birthday and she drew a picture in each respective box. I wrote in to call grandma genius on Easter Sunday!

Naturally I cried all the way home, mourning my Toni's absence.

I am active in NAMI but still need to take antidepressants which doesn't stop me from crying anyway; this is situational depression, not clinical. I find some solace in writing, drawing, talking to Dana, Michael and all my supportive friends.

I spent 2014 Christmas in California with Dana, Nelson, Michael and Melissa. It was special and important to be together.   Easter I spent alone, depressed and crying. This is an eternal void.

MAY 11, 2015

I finally read all of Toni's letters from when she was in college.   I read all my cards from Dana and Michael. It reinforced the wonderful relationship we all experienced. I was glad I read them, even though I cried. I was beginning to doubt my mothering skills. There was nothing but love and thank you in all the letters and cards.

The saddest one was a letter from Toni which she wrote: " I hope I have a relationship with my children like we have!" So many tears, so many.

Yesterday was Mothers Day. I bought her flowers and balloons and put them by my memorial magnolia tree. I asked my son-in-law what they were doing. He was spending the day with my grand-daughter and his girlfriend at the beach. He admitted it would be a difficult day and just wanted to make it a children day.

All I could answer was "So be it". I sent a picture of the flowers and balloons and wrote to him, "just a suggestion." I didn't ask if he did it. some things are better not knowing.

I received a wonderful touching letter from Dana on mothers day plus a beautiful card from her and Nelson. Nelson wrote me a personal letter some time ago which was so meaningful and caring, no occasion, just love.

Michael and Melissa told me to wait till we talked on mothers day to open my gift. I actually cooperated. I slowly opened my gift while we were on face time.

A SONOGRAM OF MY NEW GRANDCHILD. NEW BEGINNING!

How is it possible to be crying with joy and grief at the same time? I know a higher being is telling me I have more to accomplish and enjoy. I will never stop grieving for Toni but must find joy in the living.

MAY 13-16, 2015

I was having my routine Wednesday morning coffee with my friends. I felt jittery, just not right. I asked my friend Marilyn to take me to my doctor who immediately sent me to the ER! I was trying to wean off Klonipin which lowered my seizure threshold! I had a true seizure in the ER and naturally was admitted to the hospital. Another MRI, another adjustment of medications, another medical bill! All I wanted was to go home and have my Dana with me.

Dana came and along with my friend Terry came with me for my neurology check up. It is so difficult seeing yourself through your child's frightened eyes. You're supposed to be the rock, the glue of the family, the strength! Dana finally understood the implications of my illness after an excellent explanation from the PA.

JULY 2015. DREADING AUGUST

I moved into a small villa/apartment, and the closing on my house is supposed to be in September. I am still waiting for disability. The lawyer said it may take a year. How can I continue to be a critical care nurse when I have to set alarms to take my own meds, and God forbid I have another seizure. I am quite forgetful as well.

No one can take your grief away. It will never leave but I am learning to accept what is. It hurts and it always will.

I found out July 9th my new grandchild is a boy, due in December. A moment of joy. Melissa's pregnancy is going well, and Michael and her moved to Kansas City to be close to Melissa's family.

I hope to make a difference in the stigma and knowledge needed for mental health reform. I started this book two years ago.

AUGUST 21, 2015

Today Toni would have been 38 years old. I went to the beach at sunrise and released balloons to heaven for her. My goal today was to finish this book for her!

Thank You

I have been blessed with the most amazing support system. During Toni's demise my children Dana and Michael, their spouses and all my friends and family that were so understanding and there for me and my children. A special thanks to Donna and Vicki, my nieces, who gave so much love and support.

People open up when they find out about your situation. There were people I knew for years and never knew they experienced a suicide in their family.

There are those who avoid you because just don't know what to say. Here's my advice: SAY SOMETHING, ANYTHING. A simple, "I'm thinking of you but I don't know what to say." Don't ignore the situation; it doesn't go away.

I hope I'm around to be a positive influence for my children and grandchildren for many more years: that's my inspiration, that's what Toni would want.

LOVE AND HUGS,

DENISE aka PENNI

There has been an increase of 60% in suicides in the last 45 years. The age group younger. Suicide is now among the three leading causes of death ages 15-44 (male and female). Suicide attempts are up 20%: information from Befriends Worldwide. In 2014 there were 1,892 veteran suicides.

Treatment Advocacy Center Study reveals severely mentally people are likely to be in jails, not hospitals. According to James Pavle, executive director: "With little exception, incarceration has replaced hospitalization of thousands of individuals with severe mental illness in every single state."

There are so many emotions: grief, guilt, anger, devastation, surviving... NO: enduring, tolerating, tenacity, we strive. Why? We all have our reasons. Mine are two wonderful children and my grand-daughter and future grandchildren, not to mention keeping the memory of my Toni alive.

We need to be proactive. We alone can only know the concoction of emotions that are indigestible to us that no Prilosec or Nexium can cure. Everyone has pain, different degrees, different expressions to emote their pain. Some of us need to be alone, some need a host of people even if there is just silence. Every family has potential for underlying mental problems. Let's face it, Ozzie and Harriet do not exist.

We need input on where to find updated information. Good book resources, the internet, on how we can get involved. Let our sorrow have some purpose. We all know mental health care needs an extreme makeover. We all know how to get in touch with our local and state representatives. The internet is the greatest tool we have now to get our point across. We just have to watch the news and see how uncontrolled our world has become. People get involved when it hits home. I was no different. If and when it it hits, it's devastating beyond words. I dealt with it at work, but that wasn't going to happen to me!

Let's shine our own light; be a beacon in the darkness. It's about time we look at mental illness like we look at any chemical imbalanced induced disease process'. Knowledge is key. Go to the library, go on line. There are many support groups that need funding. Educate yourself, don't let it hit home!

REFERENCES

DR. E. KUBLER-ROSS

"WHEEL OF LIFE"

"LIFE AFTER DEATH"

"WORKING IT THROUGH"

"ON DEATH AND DYING"

"ON CHILDREN AND DEATH"

DR. BRIAN WEISS

"MANY LIVES, MANY MASTERS"

DR. K. JAMISON

"THE UNQUIET MIND"

"NIGHT FALLS FAST"

CARLA FINE

"NO TIME TO SAY GOODBYE, SURVIVING SUICIDE OF A LOVED ON"

JOHN F. BAGETT

"FINDING THE GOOD IN GRIEF"

HOPE EDELMAN

"MOTHERLESS DAUGHTERS, THE LEGACY OF LOSS"

LEND ME YOUR HOPE

Lend me your hope for a while I seem to have mislaid mind. Hold my hand and hug me. Listen to my ramblings, recovery seems so far, distant. The road to healing seems like a long and lonely one.

Lend me your hope for awhile I seem to have mislaid mine. Stand by me, offer me your presence, your heart and your love. Acknowledge my pain, it is so real and ever present I am overwhelmed with sad and conflicting thoughts.

Lend me your hope for a while. A time will come when I will heal and I will share my renewal, hope, and love with others.

Author unknown

ORGANIZATIONS FOR MENTAL HEALTH

NAMI.ORG: NATIONAL ALLIANCE OF MENTAL ILLNESS

AFSP: AMERICAN FOUNDATIONF FOR SUICIDE PREVENTION

AMERICAN ASSOCIATION OF SUICIDOLOGY: WASHINGTON, D.C. 202-237-2280

FRIENDS FOR SURVIVAL: SACRAMENTO, CA 916-392-0664, 800-646-7322

AMERICAN SUICIDE FOUNDATION: NY, NY 212-410-1111

HEARTBEAT: COLORADO SPRINGS, CO 719-596-2575

SUICIDE PREVENTION ADVOCACY NETWORK: MARIETTA, GA. 770-998-8819

RAY OF HOPE: IOWA CITY, IA 319-933-9890

THE LINK COUNSELING CENTER: ATLANTA, GA 404-356-9797

You can help other families avoid a tragic loss like mine. Please make a donation to the Go Fund Me fund raiser campaign started by my son Michael:

#tomorrowfortoni

All donations will go to mental health research.

ABOUT THE AUTHOR:

Born in New York and educated in Catholic Schools, Penni went on to become an RN in 1970. She worked at Albert Einstein Hospital for thirteen years, the last four in the PACU where ECT for depressed patients was performed.

Penni moved to Florida with her two beautiful daughters, Toni and Dana, with Michael in vitro. She began work in the ICU within a community hospital and then transferred to PACU for her last years there.

Penni obtained a job in the ICU at Community hospital in Davie, Florida. She quickly transferred to the PACU as soon as possible, which became her passion.

Divorced in 1993 and moved to Martin County, Florida. Again seeking a job in PACU.

Being a nurse you deal with mental anguish on a daily basis no matter what unit you work. The fear of illness, surgery, loss of control, treatment, has to be dealt with with compassion and understanding. Even the happy maternity wards have their stresses of dealing with new mothers fears.

Penni retired early due to a brain tumor after her daughter's suicide and has found a need to be proactive in mental health education.

End

A Letter From President Obama

THE WHITE HOUSE

WASHINGTON

August 19, 2014

Ms. Denise Funaro
Palm City, Florida

Dear Denise:

Thank you for writing. I have heard from many men and women whose lives have been touched by mental illness, and I am deeply saddened to hear about the loss of your daughter and the pain you have experienced.

The needs of people with mental illnesses have gone unaddressed for far too long. Since the first White House Conference on Mental Health over a decade ago, doctors and researchers have made extraordinary progress in diagnosing and treating mental illnesses, and promoting mental health. Yet, many families still lack access to the treatments and resources needed to help their loved ones recover.

As a longtime supporter of mental health parity, I recognize we must do more to improve services for individuals and families. My Administration has coordinated health forums around our country, bringing together citizens, health care professionals, and elected officials to discuss solutions for better care. We have also taken an important step by funding biomedical and behavioral research grants at the National Institute of Mental Health.

It is up to all of us to know the signs of mental health issues and lend a hand to those who are struggling. Shame and stigma too often leave people feeling like there is no place to turn. We need to make sure they know that asking for help is not a sign of weakness—it is a sign of strength. Together, we must overcome the fear and misunderstanding that surround mental illnesses so more Americans can live out their dreams and achieve their greatest potential.

For more information on mental health assistance and health care reform, visit www.MentalHealth.gov or www.HealthCare.gov.

Again, thank you for writing. Please know you and your loved ones are in my thoughts and prayers.

Sincerely,

71

www.ingramcontent.com/pod-product-compliance
Lightning Source LLC
Chambersburg PA
CBHW071229280526
45787CB00002B/858